MY TALL HANDSOME

The Mineral Point Poetry Series

Tanka & Me   Kaethe Schwehn
My Seaborgium   Alicia Rebecca Myers
Fair Day in an Ancient Town   Greg Allendorf
My Tall Handsome   Emily Corwin

MINERAL POINT POETRY SERIES   NO. 4
Kiki Petrosino, Editor

MY TALL HANDSOME
Emily Corwin   poems

Brain Mill Press · Green Bay, Wisconsin

Copyright © 2016 by Emily Corwin. All rights reserved.

Published in the United States by Brain Mill Press.
ISBN 978-1-942083-34-4

Cover photograph © Courtney Kalmbach.
Cover design by Stray King Design.
Interior illustration by Ann O'Connell.
Interior design by Williams Writing, Editing & Design.

www.brainmillpress.com

The Mineral Point Poetry Series, number 4.

Published by Brain Mill Press, the Mineral Point Series is edited by Kiki Petrosino. In odd years, the series invites submissions of poetry chapbooks around a theme. In even years, the editor chooses a full collection.

Contents

Foreword *xi*

bramble scratch *1*

ceremony *9*

pretty pretty princess vs. the underworld *17*

Author's Acknowledgments *35*

About the Author *37*

Credits *39*

Foreword

"I am perfectly hideous, you are perfectly hunky," declares the speaker of Emily Corwin's *My Tall Handsome,* and somehow the reader feels queasy at both assessments of "perfection." Corwin's poems traffic in the fairy-tale language of love—kisses, tiaras, crystals, and glass coffins fill these pages—but this work is really a meditation upon (one might even say *a furious romp through*) the darkness and decay that underlie such fantastical visions. The "hunk" in these poems is not merely the "handsome prince" of legend, but all our tactile, fleshy, and fallible bodies drawn together by love in an imperfect world.

The opening piece, "bramble patch," is a multipart meditation on the concept of "happily ever after" as imagined in traditional *faerie*. In this poem, we seem to glimpse two lovers in the midst of a power struggle that feels like the inevitable, yet-unwritten epilogue of *Cinderella* or *Snow White*. The speaker and her beloved "tall handsome" make a wandering life in the dark woods, a landscape sadly absent of helpful magical creatures (they meet "blackbird[s] and hobgoblin[s]" instead). And rather than arriving at their "castle in the clouds," this couple must "knock [their] heads dizzy on a tree bough / bark strung with baby shoes and ribbon." They bicker and separate amid these now-corrupt symbols of happy marriage, and the speaker is left with her "dull rage flickering" as her beloved "stand[s] far away in a red coat / watch[ing her] with a telescope."

These poems are unabashed in their enjoyment of the grotesque, but there is always intentionality behind Corwin's choice of imagery. Her speaker is inextricably, even ecstatically, bonded to her "tall handsome" lover, but she struggles to share the language of her rich inner life within the bounds of this relationship. What language is public? What is private? What tokens, allusions, and talismans belong only to the ardent pair? Some of the most striking images in this series emerge when the speaker contemplates her ambivalence about the language surrounding traditional marriage. Take this moment from "pretty pretty princess vs. the underworld":

> I walk in a chiffon mermaid spell
> I walk in the room with
>   a white swan glued against my back
>
>   girl in the moon with the glitter tongue ravaging
>
> I sip the goblet down, tip it upside down,
>
>   wear it as a hat

Here, the commercial "spell" of wedding-dress language becomes a means of transformation for the speaker. She transforms into a "chiffon mermaid," delicate as she walks toward her beloved in what is, perhaps, an otherworldly wedding ceremony. The overall image casts the reader in the role of observant wedding guest who witnesses, as the bride passes, the horrific "white swan glued against [her] back." This image recalls the albatross of Coleridge's *Rime of the Ancient Mariner*, as both birds appear to symbolize guilty burdens. As the swan traditionally is associated with music and poetry, its appearance here may represent the speaker's guilt at the prospect of leaving art-making behind for marriage.

But in the next couplet, the speaker can't resist her impulse to "ravage" with her "glitter tongue," to overturn goblets and societal expectations. "We snap a sugarplum, slap the guts into our gums," she later observes. There is a festive productivity in the violent "snapping" and "slapping." The sibilant *s* sounds draw us farther into an underworld ruled by an imagination that glories in the making and shattering of things. Corwin shows us that there is just as much magic in a destroyed sugarplum as in a whole one; in fact, we cannot contemplate the coming together of a love match without also thinking about decay, corruption, and eventual disunion.

Ultimately, these poems are for anyone who wants love poetry to feel like an adventure, like a journey through an interior landscape. Corwin's poems show us danger in the hydrangeas growing inside a ribcage; she charms us with mirrors, candlesticks, and magic teeth. These poems are intoxicating in a very wicked way. "I will devour you," her speaker asserts. You'd better believe it.

> Kiki Petrosino
> Editor, Mineral Point Poetry Series

MY TALL HANDSOME

bramble scratch

The woods   tall hush

here, a dull rage flickering

           pricks my pretty dress.

  This is where we snuff the candles out

  bury the toys

           cracked

  pick acorns

           swing our wicker baskets

  bring our nets

           bring our knives—

        the beastie glides

    sharpens a black snaggle

           tooth on mountain side.

Back to the bramble patch, my sleep-head twirling

    black bird and hobgoblin   fearsome

      they ring around these rosy toes of mine.

You stand far away   in a red coat

             watch me with a telescope.

I sink, cranky   into the acre mud

my little candy heart
      throwing sticks.

Don't wake the sleeping minnow

      tiptoe in the river bed.

    We knock our heads   dizzy on a tree bough

bark strung with baby shoes and ribbon

        gather hedge apples in our aprons

our tracks sticky
     bread crumbs—butter white

a wisp of sugar and woodsmoke.

         Let's find the gumdrop lady
           take all the candy

   tuck body over belly fat

    and roll back down the cliffsides.

Sugar maple glassy like

        cold microscope slide

my blood vessel spilt over the corn husk, crusty

        chill running up the spinal cord stiff—

        a scarecrow pole

          crows nipping a bouquet

            red buds speckle a shoulder of the road.

My corn doll climbing up a tree, she

        won't come down for dinner

            and you're off somewhere

                    milling around the yard-work

with your cotton mouth

                your skinny heart.

      Looks like   just gonna be me

                 and the mud pie
                 and the stick house

       scratching out
    a big dark scribble over my roof.

Kick off rain boots and wriggle

                        into the black acre

    take our ladles to the puddle mud

            soupy with egg shells, bee hive,

                  half a butterfly.

    When you lay me down, my eyes shut

           long cow lashes batting fast—

these are my flint chips for the fire

    keep the wolves running scared.

We should run away together

           and promise to never

              do this heart-skipping thing

              with anyone else.

The spell broken—

    we crab walk out of sleep

meet me tomorrow   in a brittle field

      the stalks dry, ash-white   rippling.

    Look for me in a gingham dress.

        I'll be holding blackberries

  and a small axe

      crooning in my arms.

ceremony

Blissed out
in the church house
I'm all gussied up

spill of rice
and bubbles
down my back.

I waltz, quite smitten
in the kitchen
tracking red
onto linoleum—

drippy little blister
from the wedding shoe
your eye so powder blue
smear of blush here
put your teeth where
the perfume stings.

My lips so terrible, sticky—
whiskey spilling over knees.

Went seeking your tuxedo
got too impatient, nearly kissed
your mouth clean off

forgot you need that smile
for the cameras.

Get down on one knee, I do
I do, I ask for you to be my groom
my black suit, my cummerbund.
Tell everyone—

they circle us, clink bubbly
and scream: *She happy,*
she glow pink, she pretty teeth.

Black trickle on the knee—
my leg drops off, one chunk
into a puddle.

Pops my cherry

and the water swollen, pulpy.

Room rolls over

and we shriek into the grass

dark bee hissing up my skirt.

Clover honey, amber rock

chunky—we drink up

his milk tooth snagged in

my belly button.

It's the last dance, folks

confetti on his lip steaming

leaves a hickey on spaghetti strap

the spiked punch scatters

sugar red on rhinestone

our heels stuck drunk in a fly trap.

Shall we shimmy off
these clothes, zippers
loose and moaning.

Your white glove
tugs flirty on my fallen hair
—blood clot, bobby pin
stippling your lap

my spiked head
aglitter. I want
your body sack.

Broken ankle—
my something blue
they lift you, tipsy
in a rocking chair.

I wave my glass, rosy
across the room.
They pass wood
between their hands

like spirit sticks
in cheer camp—
bad luck to let fall.

With a freckle in your eye,
with cologne bottle
and a bow tie, we slide
on white soggy cake

feel their wet gossip curdle,
my stomach bubble pops.

pretty pretty princess vs. the underworld

1

my tall handsome, you are always
hydrangea in my rib, popped open
always dazzle of salt on my punched lip

love of life
the he & me I will devour

we beneath black cherry tree
all fruits and crystals on your chest

you were my first body—now and always
forever and ever, in the pink bed rippling
                                        amen.

2

Being with you is heavenly, really
heavenly in the pearly slipper night

      twirling, twirling up that cocktail rum & coke magic
          that hocus pocus ballroom twinkle
              that witching hour with a long red kiss

my tall handsome and me, we gonna get hitched
   my arms pinched in beads brocade teardrop tiaras
I walk in a chiffon mermaid spell
I walk in the room with
  a white swan glued against my back

     girl in the moon with the glitter tongue ravaging
     I sip the goblet down, tip it upside down,
          wear it as a hat

  I am a new shiny thing
    and I steal you away from the hoopla hullabaloo rumpus
       to a stardust garden   I drip grapes
               into your perfect mouth

  bite your chest   find paradise   my sugar boo,
                  my muffin cake

my tall handsome—always hydrangea and dazzle of salt

always my popped rib and punched lip milky
always fruits and crystals, the black cherry tree
                      shaking

3

into the orchard, into the crabapple abracadabra
        we snap a sugarplum, slap the guts into our gums
                pulp so yellow sloppy

    I am perfectly hideous, you are perfectly hunky
    forever and ever in a stardust disaster   amen

scoop me up, my tall handsome
      take your bride, your one beloved
           to the glass coffin, to the pink bed rippling

           a snow pea stuck in the mattress
bow down to your nitpicky finicky fussy little princess

I stay up forever, can't zzzzzzz   zzzzzzz   zzzzzzzzzzzzzz
    I chase your heartbeat pitter patter
        it goes skip skippety like baby rabbit fluff

a rifle cracking the robin egg blue

you were my first body
the pink bed ripples.

I strike up the candlestick

and the smoke so mystical

I giddy up, whipping a carousel horse

across your absence

your shut-eye golden goldenrod

like dandelion wine and buttermilk hot cakes

mango honey yummm

the he & me I will devour

4

tulips   two lips   two ripples shake the pink sheet

the he & me, two cherries smooshed in a pie

two peas in a mattress

two itty bitty glitter tongues   ravaging

my tall handsome   in the tallest tower

               in the bedroom ripe with flames

             and nightingales

         lingerie

               caterpillars

                       rubies

           scones   lavender   and dead bees

and cappuccinos   soaps

                   and puppet strings   bells

ripening with valentines   oils   alphabet

               coins   and ghosts

      pink wine   shadowboxes

cough drops   witch hazel   white swan

          sequins   lightning

bedroom ripe with pomegranate   goblets

                                       ribbon

     dazzle of salt   rum & coke magic

         paradise

    hydrangea

5

    in the tallest tower
                in a chiffon mermaid spell   I sex you up
                        snow peas ripple on the pink bed
I devour you, sugar boo
you were my first body, muffin cake

        now and always, my hunky man candy
                so hot, I could bake cookies on you

    I could eat you right up   all salt dazzle butterstick
                      oatmeal spoon
        those fruits and crystals on your chest

we beneath black cherry tree
    with punched lips drunk hands glitter tongues
                    ravaging ravaging
  we cuddle buddy, we snooze off into the sunset
  forever and ever tall handsome snookums beloved amen.

6

I miss you

    misplace you

        I lose you already

my tall handsome   under the black cherry tree, shaking

        the wood sizzles with clocks rivers trumpets ropes

                the wood splits apart, gutted

      and the underworld swooshes up

      underworld feasting on your heartbeat

                pitter patter

        your gorgeous mouth, perfect hunky

        your fruits and crystals

        your long red kiss

    I miss you   misplace you   I lose you already

7

into the pit   into the black cherry tree, gutted
you vanish, radiant   somersault into

        the wet chanting abyss

and I am undone   darling   sugar cake.

I saw the black robe shrieking

I saw the one with the mirror cheek   rattling wicked   wicked

I saw him with daggers   rowboats   hooks   volcanoes

    I saw him jingle jangle there
        I saw him drag your heart across the wood

    you dash away   into the cherry tree
    you tall handsome corpse you
    dash away dash away   forever and ever in a stardust
                disaster

And I am undone. I am all tiaras lingerie glitter tongue
        smashed
                across your absence
hydrangea glowing in my diaphragm, punched lip milky

8

with my pearly slipper
    with rum & coke magic

and snow peas and a chiffon mermaid
                with my pretty princess hair

        I saddle up my carousel horse and gallop
        into the wet chanting abyss
        into the wood that sizzles and shakes

I'm crashing right behind you, darling
                into the pit swarmed with clocks and trumpets
                        choked red eyes

        clip clop I go to where the black robe shrieks
        where his mirror cheek rattles   wicked   wicked
                                across your absence

I see you rippling   in a perfect black hole
                what a bright gorgeous swirl you are

    I chase your heartbeat pitter patter
        I whiplash the glass pony and giddy up fast
                prancing into the void

                        the void ripe with flames
                        and bullets
                ginger
                        chemicals

jellyfish

and rosehips

and gasoline

salamander

needles   pepper

mosquito bites

and gargoyle

and dinosaurs

the void ripe with trumpets

and numbers

pitchfork

hooks

volcano

ripe with fruits and crystals

on your chest   my tall handsome

9

At the end of the black hole
in the wet abyss chanting, there is a chair.
And in that chair, there is a robe.
And in that robe, there is a wicked wicked cheek

        that is a mirror

he churns above me, that shrieking man

he jingle jangles, he rattles

when I gallop into the room

and you are there—gorgeous buttercup shimmer

   you are

      I want you back, sugar boo

      the black robe shrieks bloody murder

      I lay down my peace offerings—

      slipper, snow pea, grapes, teardrop tiara

          also hot cakes

          also tulips

          and candlestick

          and smoke so mystical

          and hocus pocus ballroom twinkle

      his cheek rattling always wicked

      always ravaging, insatiable

          so I lay me down

          my pretty princess hair

        my glitter tongue and white swan

           glued against my back

the black robe jingle jangles

        he cuts me up with hooks and choked red eyes

       girl in the moon—I am a shiny new thing

       I am willing to be gutted

       he picks the tasty precious bits

                 an eye

                    a tooth

                      an ovary

I will devour you

   slurps it all into his gullet so wicked   so spittle

                       drip jugular

                       ever shrieking

10

you were my first body
and your body comes back to me amen
my tall handsome with fruits and crystals glinting
   splendorous baby cake
being with you is heavenly sugar boo

I am perfectly hideous, you are perfectly hunky
        I am a hot mess   gutted little ruin

and still you pucker up
and still you clutch my gruesome face
          you mack all over me
          and it's a sparkler spell-breaking cherry
            bomb kinda kiss, amen

we blast out of the underworld
past chemicals   gasoline   salamander   trumpets

the black robe grinning wicked rattles   a farewell shriek
  and we shoot back   smack dab

into the orchard
        to the crabapple abracadabra
        in the tallest tower
        the pink sheet rippling

I laugh merrily into your neck
my punched lip, my one eye weeping paradise   amen
I am lovey dovey jubilee   forever and ever darling

you are my tall handsome, my sugar boo zombie man
and I—your broken sugarplum

love of life

        the he & me I will devour

forever and ever

                in the pink bed

            in a chiffon mermaid spell

           in my rib, popped open

            tall handsome

             beloved

           into the sunset

              amen

              amen

              amen

             hydrangea.

Author's Acknowledgments

I would first like to thank my mentors Cathy Wagner, Keith Tuma, and cris cheek. Thank you for your insights and sage wisdom, for pushing me in the best ways.

Thanks as well to the creative writing communities at Miami University and in the MFA program at Indiana University. The support of my peers has been tireless and tender.

And last, but certainly not least, a thank you to Joe Thornton—you are my best friend and best love. This collection would not have come together without your supply of affection and encouragement, your laughter, your heart so sweet.

About the Author

Emily Corwin is a Midwestern girl who loves all things pretty and spooky. She completed her MA at Miami University, where she studied poetry, and she is currently an MFA candidate at Indiana University in Bloomington. Her writing has appeared or is forthcoming in *Word Riot, Smoking Glue Gun, Midwestern Gothic, Split Rock Review,* and *The Rain, Party, & Disaster Society.*

Credits

Author	Emily Corwin
Editors	Kiki Petrosino, Ruthie Knox, and Mary Ann Rivers
Proofreader	Beaumont Hardy Editing
Cover Photography	Courtney Kalmbach
Cover Design	Stray King Design
Interior Art	Ann O'Connell
Interior Design	Williams Writing, Editing & Design

Brain Mill Press would like to acknowledge the support of the following patrons:

Noelle Adams

Rhyll Biest

Katherine Bodsworth

Lea Franczak

Barry and Barbara Homrighaus

Kelly Lauer

Susan Lee

Sherri Marx

Aisling Murphy

Audra North

Molly O'Keefe

Virginia Parker

Cherri Porter

Erin Rathjen

Robin Drouin Tuch

www.ingramcontent.com/pod-product-compliance
Lightning Source LLC
Chambersburg PA
CBHW021453080526
44588CB00009B/828